D1045667

The Woman Who Stayed

And other stories to encourage and inspire

Denny Coates

Dedication:

To my loving (and encouraging) wife, Donna.

This is a book of stories, written to encourage. Some of the stories are of Bible characters, some are from secular history and some are from my personal life. The basic facts of the stories are true, with some liberties taken as to dialogue and thought. The one exception being the story labeled as a parable.

There are thirty-one stories in the book. My suggestion would be to read them over the course of a month, one story a day.

All Scripture quotations are from the King James Version of the Bible.

I pray this book is a help to you as you read. If I can be of help to you in any way, feel free to contact me:

Pastor Denny Coates
Faith Baptist Church
8115 E. Main Street
Ottawa, Ohio 45875
419.523.3363
Email: pastordenny45875@yahoo.com

INDEX

"And that from a child thou hast known the holy scriptures, which are able to make thee wise unto salvation through faith which is in Christ Jesus." II Timothy 3:15

A Tale of Three Teachers

During his lifetime, he told some 100 million men and women how Jesus Christ could change their lives. He traveled, by some estimates, a million miles to do so. And hundreds of thousands took him at his word, and received Jesus Christ as their Savior.

All this, before there were cars, buses or planes, without the assistance of television or radio, or even a public address system.

He had barely a fifth-grade education, struggled to spell properly, was not a good reader, his grammar was terrible, he had no theological training, was never ordained, and as a youth was even refused membership in the church he attended because of his ignorance. One man who knew him then said he never met a man who knew less about the Bible. Yet few have been so used by God, not only in the field of evangelism, but also to found a boys school and a girls school for the underprivileged and to establish the Christian training school that now bears his name, the Moody Bible Institute, whose graduates have served as pastors and missionaries around the world. His name was Dwight Lyman Moody, known by his friends as DL.

He was born in 1837 in Northfield, Massachusetts, one of nine children born to an underemployed and indebted stonemason and his wife. His father died when DL was four, leaving his widow to manage alone her large family, and forcing her into bankruptcy. The creditors were merciless, even taking the kindling from the firebox. Only the dowager protection laws kept Mrs. Moody from losing their little farm. But to keep this farm going, there was much work for everyone to do and scarce time for such niceties as school.

As he grew older, he also grew more and more restive on the farm. He had ambition and drive, but limited opportunities in rural Massachusett. So he left home at the age of seventeen to seek his fame and fortune in the big city of Boston.

He had an uncle there who gave him employment in his shoe store and a place to sleep. But he had a stipulation: if DL were to stay there, he had to attend church and Sunday School with the family. And so he did.

Now let me tell you about his Sunday School teacher, the first of the three teachers referred to in the title of this story. His name was Edward Kimball, thirty years old, a dry-goods salesman. Kimball's heart was touched with the need of this young man with so little knowledge yet so much potential, so he went to see DL at the shoe store where he worked and talked with him, encouraging him to take Christ as his Savior right there in the store, and he did. Right there in the store. And he began to grow in his faith.

Seeking more business opportunities, he moved to Chicago at the age of nineteen and found employment at another shoe store, and seeking to learn and do more for Jesus Christ, he began attending a traditional church on

Sunday mornings, and a Sunday School outreach called the Wells Street Mission on Sunday afternoons. Right away he asked for a class of his own and was told they already had as many teachers as they had students. But they told him he could have his own class if he could find his own students. So the next Sunday he showed up with eighteen young roughs, thus doubling the Sunday School in one week!

But his rough young boys didn't care so much for the more formal atmosphere of the Wells Street Mission, and soon quit coming. And so DL decided to start his own Sunday School in one of the toughest parts of Chicago, appropriately named, "Little Hell." He began his school in an old freight car, and soon moved to larger quarters, a saloon that was vacant on Sunday mornings. Among those he recruited for helpers were the boys who had attended his class in the Well Street Mission. Their names may give you a little insight into their background: Red Eye, Smikes, Madden the Butcher, Jackie Candles, Giberick, Billy Blucannon, Darby the Cobbler, Greenhorn, Indian, Black Stovepipe, Old Man and Ragbreeches Cadet. All but one stayed with him faithfully.

Within a year or so they had outgrown the saloon, and began to meet in the North Market Hall. Soon their attendance grew to more than a thousand. One of their visitors in 1860, when DL was 23, was none other than the newly-elected President of the United States, a man by the name of Abraham Lincoln, who spoke to them briefly about success in life.

But in the midst of all this success, DL had a problem. He was uncouth, uneducated, quick-tempered and impulsive, and ... alone. But there was this Sunday School teacher he had met. (She would be the second teacher of the three mentioned in the title.) She was one of the teachers at the Wells Street Mission. He was taken right away with her beauty and character, but little did he know at the time of their meeting (he was 20, she was 15), that she was all the things he was not. She was the calm to his storm, the studied to his impulsive, the patient to his hurried, the learned to his ignorance, and ...the answer to his prayers. They married when he was 25 and she was 19. Next to coming to know Christ, he considered her the best thing that ever happened to him. And she was.

Now you need to know that, even though Moody's Sunday School had been a great success, with an attendance of over 1,000 each week, it was only part-time work for DL. Monday through Friday he was very much engaged in the shoe business, had also been buying and selling land, and was getting involved in other business ventures as well. He was considered an up and coming mover and shaker in young Chicago.

And his Sunday School was not a very organized outreach. To be honest, it seemed mostly bedlam, with some learning, hopefully, occurring. And the earnest Gospel message that would so mark his later work was not yet developed. To use his own words, "There was no harvest."

Now let me tell you of the third Sunday School teacher. He taught a class of young teen girls, and they must have been a handful. One Sunday DL was asked to take his class for him, the teacher being ill. It was not a positive experience. The girls had no respect for Moody or his teaching. He said later, "I felt like opening the door...telling them all to go home and never come back." You would wonder why such girls would even come to a Sunday School in the first place.

One day their teacher paid a call on DL. The doctor had told him that his health could not stand living along Lake Michigan in Chicago and he would have to move away, back to his native New York state, and even then he may not survive. But the teacher was concerned about more than just his health; he was concerned about the girls of his class, and about their eternal destinies. Moody suggested he call on them one by one and tell them how he felt, and offered to go with him.

And so DL and teacher number three went to see the girls. After talking to the girls one at a time, the teacher's concern for them overcame their natural hardness. This time there was no laughing in the face, as tears stood in their eyes, and they opened their hearts to Christ, one girl at a time in one home at a time, until every girl in that class had become a Christian. Shortly thereafter, the teacher left Chicago on a train bound for New York, being seen off by DL and the girls from his class, many of them in tears.

But even though this teacher left Chicago, the experience with his class did not leave DL. As he thought about that teacher and all those girls...in his own words, "And then God opened my eyes." He must make this the chief work of his life-this talking to people about Christ. So he quit his job, gave up his promising business career and began an adventure that would ultimately touch millions around the world. At first it was one person at a time, working with the Chicago YMCA, then serving as a chaplain on the front lines during the Civil War. One thing led to another, and soon he was addressing thousands, always with the same message: You can find new life in Christ.

So when you see DL Moody in heaven, and have a chance to talk with him face to face and hear firsthand how God worked in his life, don't be surprised if he looks you in the eye and says with a smile, "You know none of this would have happened if it had not been for my Sunday School teachers!"

"For he shall give his angels charge over thee, to keep thee in all thy ways." Psalm 91:11

Broken Down on the Interstate

My brother, Darrell, and his wife, Reba, had recently relocated to Grayson, Kentucky, where he had taken a position teaching math at Kentucky Christian University. He had bought a late-model Chevy sedan from a member of the church he attended and was looking forward to a week of vacation, planning to drive to Florida so he and Reba could see her brother and her brother's family who lived in the Clearwater area. Now this car had been wrecked in a previous life, but had been repaired and renewed; it looked great and drove well.

And so they headed down I-75, through Kentucky and Tennessee without issue, but somewhere in southern Georgia, the motor began making a strange noise which kept getting louder. Darrell thought it wise to get off the interstate and took an exit that looked promising. As he approached the end of the off-ramp, the engine died, but he was able to coast into the parking lot of a convenience store. He tried to restart the engine, but it would not start.

He walked into the store and was prepared to ask the clerk for assistance, when a man walked up and offered to help. He was a local fellow who knew a good mechanic and would be glad to drive Darrell over and introduce him, an offer Darrell was glad to accept. Darrell had second thoughts, however, when he approached the passenger door of the man's pickup truck, for there on the seat of the truck to greet him was a pit bull. Now the pit bull is a scary-looking breed, but this one was wagging his tail, which was encouraging, and so he opened the door and found that this was, indeed, one friendly dog that was glad to make Darrell's acquaintance, and proved it with lots of kisses to the face.

They drove without incident to the friend's garage, but it was closed. The new friend drove Darrell back to the convenience store, helping him locate a Chevy dealer and a tow truck. Before the friend left, he handed Darrell his business card and told him to give him a call if further need arose. The Chevy dealer proved to be across the interstate from a motel, so they stopped at the motel first, got a room, unpacked the car and got Reba settled in, then towed the car to the dealership.

The dealer said he would be glad to attend to the car, but as it was getting close to quitting time, he would have to wait until morning for a diagnosis of what was wrong. The car was left in the parking lot and Darrell walked back to the motel. He and Reba ate supper and stayed overnight, wondering what was going to happen and what was wrong with their car and how much it was going to cost to get their car back in running order.

They ate breakfast the next morning, waiting a bit to give the dealership guys time to look at the car. He walked over and saw that the car was still sitting where the tow truck had left it, a sure sign that nothing had been done. He approached the service manager, who sent a mechanic over to check things over. Darrell was standing beside the car, watching and listening as the man turned the ignition key. Nothing. The mechanic looked at my brother and said, "You need a new engine."

Now Darrell is not a mechanic, but he knew enough about cars to know that there can be lots of reasons a car won't start, and he thought that perhaps it would be wise to get a second opinion before paying the several thousand dollars a new engine would cost. And so he called the number on the business card given him the day before, and his pit bull-owning friend reappeared. The car was towed to a local garage the man familiar to, and the problem was found. It was the transmission. The car was left to be repaired, and Darrell rented a car. They checked out of the motel and resumed their drive to Florida, where they enjoyed several days visiting with Reba's brother and his wife.

They left Florida, returned to the garage and their now-repaired car, and drove back to Kentucky. Evidently the diagnosis had been correct, as they had no further trouble with the car.

Darrell thought it providential that things had worked out the way they had, and so related the story to his pastor. The pastor felt this made a good story (pastors are always looking for a good story), so during the Sunday evening church service he related how things had worked out for my brother and his wife. After church, the man who had sold the car to Darrell approached him (he was present in the service and had heard the story) and asked if that was the same car he had sold him. After hearing that it was, he pulled out his checkbook and paid half the cost of the repair.

Then Darrell remembered the stranger with the pit

bull, and thought it would be good to call him and tell him how things had worked out and to thank him again for his help. He pulled out the man's business card and dialed. The operator answered: "I'm sorry, the number you have dialed is not a working number."

Ask, and it shall be given you; seek, and ye shall find; knock, and it shall be opened unto you: For everyone that seeketh receiveth; and he that seeketh findeth; and to him that knocketh it shall be opened." Matthew 7:7,8

Prayers & Droughts & Tow-trucks

I can still see it in my mind, our almost new car being towed away on that summer Sunday morning. It was Father's Day, 1988, thirty years ago. 1988 was the year of the drought.

In our part of the world, we remember time by the big weather events – the flood of '07, the blizzard of '78, the tornado outbreak of '74, the drought of '88. The drought that year was one of the worst in history, affecting not just Ohio but 39 other states. Hundreds would die before it was over, this most costly natural disaster since the Dust Bowl of the 1930's. It was dry and it was hot. To put the heat into context, in our part of Ohio a normal summer brings six 90-degree days. That year there were more than forty.

We were a young family of four that hot summer of '88'. My wife and I and our two daughters, ages six and three. We were in the process of planting a church, having begun in the fall of 1985 with two other couples and their children. Growth was coming, but slowly, and our personal finances were rather tight. We had a small air conditioner that cooled one bedroom, but the rest of the house was sweltering. So what did we do? We prayed and asked God for help.

It was about nine o'clock in the morning and we had just finished breakfast. My wife and daughters were getting ready for Sunday School which began at ten. I was standing in the kitchen, doing what, I don't remember, when I heard the loudest crash. I looked out the kitchen door which faces the brick street we live on, and there was our car, which I had parked on the street the night before, now sitting at an odd angle, partly knocked into the yard, noticeably closer, rather forlorn.

And there was our neighbor's daughter, who had been on her way home from her church and had misjudged the distance somehow between her front bumper and our rear one, and thus there was an unplanned encounter between her car and ours. Things did not look good. The police were called and a tow truck summoned to haul our car away.

And now, to make a long story shorter, within a day or two an insurance adjuster appeared, having driven down from Toledo. It took a couple of visits, and some negotiations, but soon he was writing out a check made payable to us and the body shop doing the repair. It was about this time that the owner of the body shop informed us that if we were willing to use a "clip," that is, the back half of a wrecked car welded onto the front half of our wrecked car, we could save several hundred dollars. Now the first thing I thought of was that episode of Candid Camera where the trick car comes apart and the folks in the back seat appear in the rear view mirror, but the body shop owner assured me that such would not be the case. And he was right — our family stayed together, literally!

And guess what we did with the money left over? We went to Sears and bought a beautiful big window air conditioner, big enough to cool the whole downstairs of our house. It was not the way we expected our prayers to be answered, but God surely took care of the problem for us. "Call unto me, and I will answer thee, and show thee great and mighty things which thou knowest not." Jeremiah 33:3

"But Jesus beheld them, and said unto them, With men this is impossible; but with God all things are possible." Matthew 19:26

Attempting the Impossible

They said we didn't have a prayer.

The time was late spring, 1944. Adolph Hitler and the German army had "blitz-krieged" their way across Europe, conquering country after country, stopping only when they reached the English Channel. The logistical problems of crossing that arm of the North Atlantic had been too great to overcome, so England seemed safe for the moment from invasion.

In the interim, England and her allies, including millions of servicemen and women from the United States, were massing troops and supplies, preparing for the invasion of German-controlled Europe. D-Day. And that same English Channel stood in the way.

To try to transport and land hundreds of thousands of servicemen, to coordinate the thousands of ships required and the hundreds of planes involved, plus deal with the often-difficult weather and sea conditions, not to mention the fact that the Germans knew what was coming and were entrenched and prepared—why it seemed beyond believable that we could or would attempt such a task.

Much has been made of the subsequent invasion, telling of the internal conflicts and the bloody beaches, where planners got it right and where expediters got it wrong. Some flew in silently in their gliders, while others waded through bloody beaches facing machine-gun fire every step of the way.

But there was another dimension to this landing that seems to have been forgotten. President Roosevelt was concerned that Americans at home would support this effort with prayer, and so he wrote a prayer that was printed and distributed across the nation on June 6, 1944, asking for God's help and encouraging us to pray:

"Almighty God: Our sons, pride of our Nation, this day have set upon a mighty endeavor, a struggle to preserve our Republic, our religion, and our civilization, and to set free a suffering humanity. Lead them straight and true; give strength to their arms, stoutness to their hearts, steadfastness in their faith. They will need thy blessings..."

And across America, we prayed. In Columbus, Ohio, Mayor Rhodes called for city-wide cooperation in this prayer emphasis, and asked for the entire city to stop at 7:30 that evening and pray. Air raid sirens and whistles sounded for the five minutes before so people could prepare to pray. And at 7:30, traffic ceased so motorists could pray—some even kneeling in the street. Pedestrians stopped for the moment, then many headed to churches so they could join others in prayer for our men in uniform.

Later that evening, over the radio, President Roosevelt led the nation in the prayer he had written. Some estimated 80 to 100 million people lifted their voices as one across the nation.

He closed his prayer with these words: "Give us

strength too...And let our hearts be stout... to bear sorrows that may come...And O Lord, give us faith. Faith in Thee; Faith in our sons; Faith in each other. With Thy blessing, we shall prevail..".

And God answered in ways beyond imagining, and the war was ultimately won.

We did have a prayer after all.

And now, as our nation faces issues that seemingly have no solutions, such as the breaking up of the family, and the ever-growing threat of radical terrorism, maybe it is time to pray again.

"Yea, though I walk through the valley of the shadow of death, I will fear no evil: for thou art with me; thy rod and thy staff they comfort me." Psalm 23:4

There's Got To Be a Morning After

From the years 1989 through 2006 I had the privilege of serving as a volunteer, a basic EMT, on the Ottawa-Glandorf (Ohio) EMS squad. During those almost 17 years of service, I answered thousands of emergency and non-emergency calls but remember the details of very few. But I do remember what happened one day in August in the year 2000. The family has kindly given me permission to tell you about it.

It was a Thursday afternoon. I was busy doing my normal pastor-type things. I was not serving on the main EMS crew that day, but had my radio with me in case something came up while the scheduled crew was busy. Something did.

"Attention, Ottawa EMS back-up squad, Attention, Ottawa EMS back-up squad. You have a code situation at 5146 US 224. Repeat. You have a code situation at 5146 US 224. Medic 300 will meet you there. CPR is in progress."

I was at the station house in minutes and answered the call.

"Squad 101 to Putnam County. Received your call. I am en-route."

I pulled the ambulance from the station and headed east, lights flashing, siren blaring. Another EMT, a paramedic named Sue, radioed that she was also on the way in her own vehicle, and would meet us at the scene.

As quickly as I could I covered the five mile distance to the location given by the dispatcher. I pulled in o the drive, noticing that the Medic 300 vehicle was already there. That meant that JoAnne, our full-time paramedic, must be inside assessing the situation.

"Squad 101 to Putnam County. We are on the scene."

I grabbed what equipment I thought would be needed and headed in to the house. I saw a man, whom I would learn later was Bob, on the floor. The first thing I noticed about him was his color: gray, ashen gray. CPR was being performed by a woman, his wife, I was told. He was not responding.

"Quick, get the heart monitor out of the ambulance," JoAnne ordered.

I did as I was told. The heart monitor advised that Bob's heart had stopped and that immediate application of the AED paddles was needed. JoAnne readied the paddles.

"All clear!" We were always advised to not be touching the person being shocked to avoid being shocked ouselves. "Clear," I responded.

The button was pushed; the electric current delivered, his body jerked in response. The monitor was checked; his heart was beating again! And not only that, but Bob began conversing with us, almost as if nothing out of the ordinary had happened.

We loaded Bob into the ambulance. I was driving, with paramedics JoAnne and Sue in the back with the patient. His wife, whose name I learned was MaryJo, also climbed in the back of the ambulance. I told her she would need to ride up front so she would not interfere with Bob's care. JoAnne told me to let her stay in the back, as MaryJo was a nurse and could help with treatment.

Now I need to pause in this re-telling to give you a bit of the "back-story," as related to me by MaryJo. The night before this fateful day, Bob and MaryJo had had an argument over her going to church to a prayer meeting. It had left MaryJo quite upset, not just over the argument, but over the general state of their marriage; it was not a happy home.

It was fitting that they should argue over a prayer meeting, because the crux of the matter was this: MaryJo was a Christian, and Bob was not. She knew that if Bob would just open his heart to Jesus Christ, their marriage would be transformed. But how to get him to this point? She had tried to talk to him. She had tried to reason, had left written notes to get his attention. But he was unmoved; the situation seemed hopeless.

And so as MaryJo met with her prayer group that night before, and shared some of her heartache, the tears flowed freely down her face. One of the women in the group took her hand and prayed the following: "Lord, do whatever it takes to make Bob realize he needs to accept Christ as his Lord and Savior." No one knew how quickly that prayer would be answered.

So now, back to the ambulance. While the two

paramedics were working on Bob, before we left the scene headed for the hospital, MaryJo knelt down by Bob's face and said, "Bob, do you know that if you repented of your sins and asked Jesus in your heart, he would come into your heart and make you a new man? Have you ever done that?"

Bob closed his eyes and was silent for a moment. Then he opened his eyes, looked at his wife, and said, "I have now."

MaryJo said that at that moment I began singing, "What a mighty God we serve." I honestly don't remember doing so. But I was amazed at the events of that afternoon.

We proceeded to the hospital, where Bob was admitted, but no heart problem could be pin-pointed. And so Bob was released, and was well for a while. But then he suffered another episode and open-heart surgery was recommended. He died in the recovery room after the surgery, never regaining consciousness.

About two months transpired from that Thursday in August to the fatal day of the surgery. But during those two months, MaryJo relates that her husband Bob was like a new man, finding delight each day in learning what a difference it makes when a man knows Christ. And their marriage became a truly happy one, where each of them tried so hard to please the other, and both together knew that by doing so, they were pleasing God.

One thing they would do together each day was pray and study using a prayer calendar as a guide, called, "365 Names for God." MaryJo related how uncanny it was that so often that the scripture used in that prayer calendar would perfectly fit the circumstances of their day.

Bob's open-heart surgery was scheduled early in the morning, so they had their devotions together the night before. Bob was in the hospital bed, MaryJo by his side, and he asked her to look at the prayer calendar.

"Who is God tomorrow?" he asked. And the scripture for that day was John 11:25,26.

"I am the resurrection and the life; he that believeth in me, though he were dead, yet shall he live. And whosoever liveth and believeth in me shall never die."

"And suddenly there was with the angel a multitude of the heavenly host praising God, and saying, Glory to God in the highest, and on earth peace, goodwill toward men."

Luke 2:13,14

Dark Christmas

Christmas, "it's the most wonderful time of the year!" Or so the song goes. But for Henry, the light had gone out of the holiday. In a freak accident, his wife had been horribly burned, and he had been there and tried to help extinguish the flames, but not in time to save her life. All he had succeeded in doing was to burn himself so severely that his face would be scarred for the rest of his life, scars he covered with a full beard. Too bad the beard couldn't cover the scars on his heart.

It was 1863, and adding to his misery was this infernal war. Civil war. There was nothing civil about it! Every day the papers told of more carnage; hadn't there been enough death and dying? And to top it off, his son, Charles, his first-born, was fighting in that war, a war he didn't approve of, and what's even worse, he had signed up and left without even telling his father good-bye.

Maybe he would work on that Christmas piece he was writing. That would get his mind off missing his wife and worrying about his son. He was thinking about the words of the angels the night Christ was born, about peace on earth and goodwill to men, and how Christians had celebrated this event year after year.

And then the telegram came. It arrived December 1. Charles had been wounded in action. Shot in the shoulder. Bullet missed the spinal cord by one inch. Would he be paralyzed? What about infection? Gangrene was a constant threat for those wounded amidst the squalor of the battlefield. Would Charles survive?

And what about Henry? Would he survive? Henry was a Christian; would his faith survive? Was God in control or not? What an awful Christmas this was turning out to be!

But Henry chose to keep trusting God. After all, isn't the very heart of the meaning of faith that we choose to keep believing even when things don't work out the way we had hoped? That maybe God sees things that we don't, that he has a purpose and a plan even when we don't understand what that purpose might be?

And so he finished his Christmas poem, and Charles recovered from his wounds and was released from the army in 1864. The war ended in 1865, and the healing of the nation began. And a man with a funny name, Jean Baptiste (John the Baptist) Calkin, took the words of the Christmas poem and set them to music. And now Henry's story is retold every year, each time we sing, "I Heard the Bells on Christmas Day," by Henry Wadsworth Longfellow.

"Christmas Bells"

I heard the bells on Christmas Day
Their old familiar carols play,
And wild and sweet

The words repeat
Of peace on earth, goodwill to men!

And thought how, as the day had come,
The belfries of all Christendom
Had rolled along
The unbroken song
Of peace on earth, goodwill to men!

Till ringing, singing on its way,
The world revolved from night to day,
A voice, a chime,
A chant sublime
Of peace on earth, goodwill to men!

Then from each black, accursed mouth
The cannon thundered in the South,
And with the sound
The carols drowned
Of peace on earth, goodwill to men!
It was as if an earthquake rent
The hearthstones of a continent,
And made forlorn
The households born
Of peace on earth, goodwill to men!

And in despair I bowed my head;
"There is no peace on earth," I said;
"For hate is strong,
And mocks the song,
Of peace on earth, goodwill to men!"

Then pealed the bells more loud and deep:
God is not dead, nor doth he sleep;
The wrong shall fail,
The right prevail
With peace on earth, goodwill to men.

Henry Wadsworth Longfellow

"And behold, there was a man named Zacchaeus, which was the chief among the publicans, and he was rich. And he sought to see Jesus who he was; and could not for the press, because he was little of stature." Luke 19:2,3

Little Donnie Warner

In the University of Michigan legendary football coach Bo Schembechler's book on leadership, he tells an interesting story of a walk-on by the name of Donnie Warner.

Donnie Warner enrolled at the University of Michigan in 1970 to study engineering. One day before school started, he dropped by the coach's office to talk to him. He told him he'd like to play Michigan football. Coach looked him over and wasn't impressed. Warner was small, maybe 170 pounds, about 5'9" tall. He asked him if he was thinking of being a running back, but Warner said no. He wanted to be an offensive lineman, a guard.

Coach Schembechler quickly discouraged him from such an idea, and described two of his offensive lineman for him as being about 6'4" or 6'5" and weighing 240 – 250 pounds. Warner replied that if he were too small for the offensive line, he'd play on the defensive line as middle guard. Coach didn't like that idea either, but Warner wouldn't be dissuaded.

Donnie Warner told him that he had attended Dearborn Divine Child High School and asked the coach if he remembered speaking there at their team banquet.

He did. And Warner asked him if he remembered how he had told them that if they set their mind on doing something, they should do it, and not let anyone talk them out of it! And Donnie had set his mind on being a Wolverine! Well, what choice did Coach Schembechler have but to let him come out for the team?

And so he did. Of course, his only playing time was on the demo team during the first few minutes of practice, and even then he was knocked flying time after time. But he didn't give up and finished the season. When Coach interviewed him at the end of the year, he congratulated him on finishing, but again tried to talk him into giving it up. He was too small – couldn't he see that now?

No, he could not. He was more determined than ever to play Michigan football and promised to work hard during the off-season to get stronger and bigger.

The next year, Donnie Warner earned a regular spot on the demo team. At the end of that season, Coach Schembechler told him he had earned his spot on the team. At the beginning of his junior year, he was placed at number three or four in the depth chart as middle linebacker.

But he was getting to be a pain in the neck during practice because he kept getting into the backfield of the offense and disrupting plays and tackling the ball carriers. And when this would happen he would celebrate and carry on so, you would have thought he'd just tackled Joe Namath. Even the coaches found that, during practice, instead of watching the offense, they would find themselves watching little Donnie Warner just to see what he was going to do.

The fall of his senior year, he was finally named the starting middle linebacker. Coach Schembechler thought it would be only temporary, but once again he had underestimated Donnie Warner. He became a vital part of a great defense of an outstanding University of Michigan team. During their first ten games, they gave up a total of 58 points. That's less than 6 points per game playing the top teams in the nation.

How did he do it? Well, first of all, he used his head, and would watch the offense during their huddle. Who was the quarterback talking to? He would get into his crouch and watch which way the offensive linemen were leaning. And then he would look at the gaps between the offensive guards and study how the center lined up. And from this little bit of detective work he would know what they were going to do; whether they would pass, run, and who would carry the ball.

And secondly, he was quick. He'd get between the guards before they knew he'd been there, or around the center in nothing flat, and there he was in the backfield, ready to wreak havoc! And he did!

His senior year the University of Michigan won ten games in a row. Their last game was against arch-rival Ohio State, which ended in a tie, and a game that Donnie Warner was not able to complete because of a knee injury.

What a player was little Donnie Warner. He didn't have the size. He didn't have the talent. But he had brains, he was quick, and, of course, he was determined. He surpassed expectations to the point that, years later, Coach Schembechler would say that Donnie Warner was the greatest player he had ever coached.

As the old proverb says: "It's not the size of the dog in the fight, but the size of the fight in the dog."

"And I will bring the blind by a way that they knew not; I will lead them in paths that they have not known: I will make darkness light before them, and crooked things straight. These things will I do unto them, and not forsake them." Isaiah 42:16

Fanny's Other Doctor

"If it hadn't been for that nutty doctor, think what she might have accomplished with her life!" Such might have been said of the famed hymn writer, Fanny Crosby, if it weren't for the simple fact that it's hard to imagine anyone accomplishing more with a life than she who wrote such beloved hymns as "Blessed Assurance, Jesus is Mine," "To God Be the Glory," "Redeemed, How I Love to Proclaim It," "All the Way My Savior Leads Me," and over 8,000 more!

A victim of the medical malpractice of a visiting doctor, Fanny was blinded from infancy. And to add to her childhood difficulty, her father died when she was only one, placing the family in difficult financial straits, and forcing her mother to seek employment as a household maid.

So how did she manage to rise from such meager beginnings in 1820 to become one of the best-known and esteemed women of the nation by the time of her death in 1915?

One simple explanation is her attitude of refusal to feel sorry for herself. Indeed, one poem she wrote at the age of eight speaks volumes:

"O what a happy soul am I!
Although I cannot see;
I am resolved that in this world
Contented I will be.

How many blessings I enjoy,
That other people don't;
To weep and sigh because I'm blind,
I cannot and I won't!"

And she was remarkably free of any malice or anger toward the no doubt well- meaning doctor that caused her to lose her sight. She felt that her blindness was actually a gift from God that enabled her to see in a way that others could not. "It was the best thing that could have happened to me. How in the world could I have lived such a helpful life had I not been blind?"

One thing that Fanny was not happy about as a child, however, was the closed door of the schools of the day to blind students. She longed to learn with the other children. And so it proved a godsend when her mother heard of a school called the New York Institute for the Blind. Fanny was almost 15 years of age when she was finally given this opportunity to learn, but she was overjoyed to be finally given the chance to get an education.

She would stay at the Institute for more than twenty years, first as a student and then serving on staff. We remember her today for her hymns, but those were all to come later in life. In her earlier years, through the auspices of the Institute for the Blind, she would appear and recite on two separate occasions before the US Congress, would get to meet and actually know personally several US presidents, especially enjoying a close friendship with Grover Cleveland, who had worked at the New York school as a teenager.

Young Fanny had two remarkable gifts – the first being a memory that enabled her to recite at length whole books of the Bible and poems written by others. Her second gift was this ability to "versify." Indeed, even at a very young age her poetry appeared in print in such leading publications as, *The Saturday Evening Post,* and the *New York Herald.* Years, even decades, before her hymns would make her a household name, she would publish several books of original poetry. She was, in a word, prolific!

And one gets the impression that such constant poetry-making was not always appreciated among the faculty at the New York Institute for the Blind. One put it this way:

> "Young Fanny is a poet
> Only problem is, she knows it;
> A little rhyme is fine,
> But not all the time!
> Perhaps in time she'll outgrow it!"

In interest of total disclosure, the above limerick was not written by a faculty member. But it is true that certain members of the staff of the school had grown weary of her poetry, so much so that she was requested to stop and take a ninety-day fast from poem-making. And if she had taken such negativity to heart, the world would be a much poorer place today. It was at this point that the "other doctor" came on the scene.

Fanny Crosby herself felt that the blindness caused by the first doctor was a blessing in disguise. Now we will learn that this encounter with the other doctor would also prove a blessing. His name was Dr. George Combe; he was a phrenologist. By today's standards we would consider him a quack. Phrenologists believed that a person's true character and abilities could be determined by feeling the bumps on the head. And when Dr. Combe got Fanny's skull in his hands, he declared her a poet, and advised the faculty to give her every encouragement. And they did! And the rest is history.

So don't be discouraged if others don't appreciate your best efforts to serve! The Lord looks on the heart and is pleased when we do our best for His glory. And you never know; you may be another Fanny Crosby waiting to be discovered! Come over here – let me look at your head…

"The Lord is my light and my salvation; whom shall I fear? The Lord is the strength of my life; of whom shall I be afraid? Psalm 27:1

God is Greater Than That

Disclaimer: the events of the following story happened a number of years ago, and some dialogue and story detail may not be exactly accurate. The basic facts of the story occurred as described.

"You mean they stood you before a firing squad?" I asked incredulously. The firing squad story was just one of several told to me by Tom Crawford, a missionary who had served 25 years in what was once the nation of Rhodesia in southern Africa, a country now known as Zimbabwe.

Both Rhodesia and the country of South Africa had been led by white minority governments, and both would be forced to change their ways. South Africa's new day was led by Nelson Mandela, who championed a peaceful transition to a representative- type government, with equal rights for all regardless of race or ethnicity.

In Rhodesia, the transition to a new government was led by a man named Robert Nugabe, and it would not be a peaceful transition, but rather a very bloody one. Ultimately the new nation of Zimbabwe would have a socialist government with very limited rights for anyone.

Caught in the middle of this process in Rhodesia/ Zimbabwe was the man I was interviewing, Tom Crawford. The year was 1981, and I was working for a youth publication at the time, and most of the stories told to me have been forgotten. But I do remember quite clearly the story of his being arrested and placed in a concentration camp, and how he had shared the gospel with an African national who was also living in the camp. He told how they had prayed together, the man becoming a Christian. A guard came over, yelling and upset that they had been talking together, and brutally stomped the man to death.

Now I don't remember if that was the reason, or if there were other offenses, but Crawford was then sentenced to die by firing squad. The squad was assembled, Crawford was blindfolded and told to stand before a wall. "Ready, Aim, Fire!" The shots rang out, but miraculously, the bullets missed, and he was unhurt. I don't know if diplomatic efforts were made by our government, but somehow he was released from the camp, allowed to reunite with his family, leave the country and come back to the USA.

The interview ended with his relating to me that he could sum up all those years of ministry with one sentence: "God is greater than that." And he went on to explain what he meant, that no matter what you are facing, it's not beyond the God of the impossible to work in ways you can't imagine, to make things work out in a great way.

And so, in thinking of those things, I wrote a little song based on that idea, illustrated by some well-known Bible stories. Check them out for yourselves in the books of I Samuel, chapter 17; and Joshua, chapter 6; and Judges chapter 7.

God is Greater Than That

"Is there not a cause?"
 I can hear David say,
As he pushes his fears
And his brothers away.
"Just give me some rocks for my sling and get back;
Our God is greater than that!"

Around and around
The Israelites went,
For to Jericho's walls,
They had been sent.
After seven times the walls tumbled flat!
Our God is greater than that!

"The sword of the Lord,"
Is what Gideon said,
As he 300 men
To the Midianites led;
I know we're outnumbered, but we cannot turn back!
Our God is great than that!

Chorus:
Our God is greater than that!
Our God is greater than that!
No mountain too tall,

No valley too low;
Our God is greater than that!

"They shall still bring forth fruit in old age; they shall be fat and flourishing." Psalm 92:14

Granny

Ask almost anyone old enough to remember to list the prominent television shows of the '60s, and "The Beverly Hillbillies," will be among those mentioned. A silly sit-com about a zany family made instantly wealthy due to the discovery of oil on their property, "The Beverly Hillbillies" featured the antics of the Clampett family, led by the widower, Jed, and his mother-in-law, Daisy Mae Moses, more commonly known as Granny.

Granny. What can you say about her? She was a woman small of stature, but big in spirit, full of fire and temper and opinion. When big Jethro, standing 6'5" tall, was caught raiding the fridge, he ran for his life when the 5'2" Granny came after him with that iron skillet! And when Granny spoke, everyone listened! She was the heart of the show and appeared in every episode throughout the nine seasons that it ran.

Her character was named for Grandma Moses, the artist who became famous only in her later years, painting well into her nineties. Originally the role of Granny was to go to Bea Benadaret, but when Irene Ryan auditioned for the part with her hair pulled back and her teeth clenched in full "Granny mode," everyone agreed Ryan was made for the part!

Born in 1902, Jessie Irene Noblitt had been in

show business almost all her life, starting at age 11 by winning a contest with a song, "Pretty Baby." She married at the age of 20, and she her husband, Tim Ryan, hit the road with a vaudeville routine similar to George Burns and Gracie Allen.

From vaudeville, they went on to radio, and she seemed at last to have hit the big time. Filling in for Jack Benny in the 1930s, touring with Bob Hope during World War II in the '40s, she seemed destined for great things. And she began acting in movies, and then television shows, but it seemed that while she was getting more opportunities in show business, the roles she was given were growing smaller. Sometimes she would be given a role so small she was not even listed in the credits.

So, in 1962, when she learned of Paul Henning's project, this proposed TV show about a bunch of hillbillies, she was glad to give it a try. What did she have to lose? She was already on the edge of show business obscurity. Little did she know that this role of Granny would catapult her into fame and fortune and make her one of the most recognizable women anywhere in the United States.

Sixty years of age; a time when most would think of retiring, but Irene Ryan was just getting started. In its first two seasons, "The Beverly Hillbillies" became the most highly watched show in the nation. And even in the last season, the show was still ranked 30[th.] Not bad at all, considering that from the very first episode the critics hated it!

And then after nine years of television stardom,

Irene realized one more dream come true. She had done vaudeville, radio, movies and television, but she had never appeared on Broadway. There was a play being cast, a musical called, "Pippin," that had a part for a grandmother that seemed perfect for Irene. The show went on to become a great hit and be nominated for 11 Tony awards, including one nomination for Irene as "Best Featured Actress in a Musical."

Her solo from that show had been released as a 45 on Motown records, and can still be heard on Youtube; the lyrics so fitting:

> "When you are as old as I, my dear
> And I hope that you never are
> You will woefully wonder why, my dear
> Through your cataracts and catarrh
> You could squander away or sequester
> A drop of a precious year
> For when your best days are yester'
> The rest'er twice as dear...
>
> Now when the drearies do attack
> And a siege of the sads begins
> I just throw these noble shoulders back
> And lift these noble chins...
>
> Oh, it's time to start livin'

Time to take a little from this world that we're given

Time to take time, cause spring will turn to fall

In just no time at all…

"Pippin" would be her last foray into show business. After less than a year in her grandmotherly role, at the age of 69, Irene suffered a stroke during a performance and died about six weeks later, leaving the legacy of a little lady with a lot of spirit who didn't want to go away quietly, but instead squeezed all she could out of the life she had been given.

"Unto me, who am less than the least of all saints, is this grace given, that I should preach among the Gentiles the unsearchable riches of Christ;" Ephesians 3:8

Had John Failed?

As John surveyed the chaotic scene resulting from Bill's failed attempt to take his own life, he surely must have felt like a failure. He knew that his dear friend had been struggling with depression and felt that God had given up on him because of it, but he had no idea it was as bad as all this.

John was a pastor in Olney, a small town in England, serving a church full of hard-working people, his first church, in fact. And he'd been delighted when Bill came to town and to his church, for William had such a mind and such a heart! They quickly became the best of friends, and could often be seen together, walking, talking and even collaborating in a writing ministry together.

The day before had been New Year's Day, the year 1779, and in church that day John had preached from I Chronicles 17:16, "Who am I, O Lord God...that thou has brought me hitherto?" The words were those of King David in response to God's goodness and grace.

This passage of scripture tells how King David wanted to build a temple for worship of the Lord God, and how the Lord refused him, and at the same time told him that, while David couldn't build him a house, the Lord would bless David greatly and would establish his kingly line forever. David's response indicates he felt very undeserving of this great grace. John certainly saw the parallels in his own life.

John was John Newton, that great Anglican preacher of the gospel, but he had not always been so saintly, and in point of fact had been a slave ship captain, that most vile of occupations. If any man did not deserve to be blessed and forgiven and chosen for preaching the gospel, it was John Newton; he truly had been a wretch of a man.

Bill was William Cowper (pronounced "cooper') a descendant of a prominent family and destined to become one of England's great poets. But at this point in his life, he was a little-known man trying to get his life together.

And as John Newton prepared his sermon in the closing days of December 1778, he put together a little poem, a hymn, to go with his sermon, which carried the idea that God does not easily give up on people and that God does not deal with us on the basis of what we deserve. He called it "Faith's Review and Expectation." He wrote this simple hymn to help his congregation understand the Bible text, and no doubt he also wrote to encourage William, who came to church that day and tried to kill himself that night. And while he lived another 27 years, he never came back to church.

Was it all a wasted effort? Newton indicated disappointment over the sermon in his diary, and the hymn he wrote was to fade into obscurity, at least for a while. It failed to become popular in England, was not even included in any of the official hymnals printed by the Anglican Church over the next 100 years. It didn't catch on, that is, in England. But in America, a man named William Walker matched the hymn to a different tune, and soon people were singing it everywhere.

"Faith's Review and Expectation" went on to become a favorite, loved around the world and sung or played at weddings and funerals and church services of every denomination. It's been called the "spiritual national anthem of America." Only we no longer refer to it by John Newton's title. We simply call it by the first words of the first verse, "Amazing Grace."

"He that is slow to anger is better than the mighty; and he that ruleth his spirit than he that taketh a city." Proverbs 16:32

Has-been Fred

Oh well, it was fun while it lasted. He had been considered a prodigy in his younger years, playing 3 instruments well, writing music the world found wonderful, staging productions with standing-room only crowds, enjoying the fame and the wealth. But now...in his fifties, on the verge of old age, just another has-been. "Has-been Fred."

And sometimes, late at night, he played the "if only" game. If only, if only the good times had lasted...if only the great ideas would still come...if only the fickle fans would still pack out his productions...if only the cast members could get along...if only his health would have held...if only he could have stayed current on his bills...if only. Maybe if things had been different, he wouldn't be "Has-been Fred."

And to be honest, some of it was his own doing. If only he had learned to control his temper! But that Italian soprano, Cuzzoni, that wouldn't listen to him! Perhaps he shouldn't have grabbed her the way he had and threatened to throw her out the window. But honestly, she was so provoking, and he was the director, the true star, back in the day, before he was, "Has-been Fred."

And in retrospect, maybe that one duel shouldn't have been fought, either. But it wasn't over nothing! It's important where the members of the orchestra sit! Fortunately for him, the point of the sword had been deflected by a steel button on his coat, or he would have been the "Dead Fred!"

And maybe he shouldn't have made such a deal about people arriving on time for performances, especially when the ones guilty of such offense were the Prince and Princess of Wales.

But now he was stricken with palsy—too much stress, the doctors said—stricken in his hands, his fingers, which would no longer cooperate. What is a musician without his hands? And then, as if things couldn't get any worse, he had been forced to file for bankrupcy! The man who had once been the best paid musician on earth! "Has-been Fred!"

If only he could get a fresh start! That last season had been a great failure. How he hated the rejection! And then one day, through the mail, some man named Janner sent him a manuscript. Janner had taken many of the references concerning Jesus as recorded in the Bible and written them out in organized fashion. And that gave Fred an idea that soon blossomed into a full production. He closed himself in at his London house and gave himself to writing music night and day for over 3 weeks. And he wrote such a piece of music, that never again would he be "Has-been Fred." Forever and after he would be known as the man who wrote "Messiah," the greatest oratorio ever, George Frederick Handel!

All he needed was a little inspiration!

"And the angel said unto her, Fear not Mary: for thou hast found favor with God. And behold, thou shalt conceive in thy womb, and bring forth a son, and shalt call his name JESUS. He shall be great, and shall be called the Son of the Highest; and the Lord God shall give unto him the throne of his father David: And he shall reign over the house of Jacob for ever; and of his kingdom there shall be no end. Then said Mary unto the angel, How shall this be, seeing I know not a man?"
Luke 1:30-34

Mary, Were You Wrong

"How can it be?" That was essentially the question the young virgin named Mary asked of the angel when told of the baby who was to be born to her, the baby that she was instructed to name, Jesus, Savior, the baby who would become king and sit on David's throne. According to the account found in the Gospel of Luke, chapter 1, this news left her troubled, and trying to understand, she asked for an explanation. She was a virgin, unmarried, and she was to give birth to the baby Jesus? How can this be? Was it wrong of her to ask?

Aren't we to blindly accept without thinking whatever we are told? To quote Mark Twain, isn't faith "believing what we know ain't so?" The passage in question would not indicate that at all, for when Mary asks for more information, she is not blasted for impertinence or lack of faith, but instead the angel explained patiently to her that the Holy Spirit would come upon her and that this baby that would become our Savior and King, would also be the Son of God.

Our Lord Jesus would grow up and teach us many things during his three years of earthly ministry. One of the dearest promises he gave, recorded in the Gospel of Matthew, chapter 7, was this, "Ask and you shall receive, seek and you shall find, knock and the door shall be opened to you." Why do we only think of this as pertaining to praying for things. Why could it not also pertain to praying for understanding God and his purposes?

Our success in finding answers to our questions would seem to depend greatly on our motive in asking. For example, in the Gospel of Matthew, chapter 2, the wise men from the East came to Jerusalem, seeking him who was born King of the Jews. According to that passage, King Herod also wanted to find him. Guess who was successful and who was not in their quest to find Jesus?

And speaking of the wise men, how many were there? How did they associate the star with the birth of Jesus? How long did their journey take? Did they travel in a caravan? Did their co-workers think them crazy for taking all that time off for their quest? How could a star shine down on just one location?

Lew Wallace was just a young boy when he first heard of the wise men who came seeking, listening at his mother's knee as she read to him from the Bible. And though he would go on to great things, becoming first a lawyer, then a state legislator in Indiana, then a soldier and ultimately a Major General during the Civil War, he never got over that fascination with the story of the wise men, even writing a short story imagining what that journey must have been like.

On a train trip to Indianapolis in 1876, he happened to run into Robert Ingersoll, also a lawyer and former officer in the Union Army. Ingersoll had made a name for himself as a great agnostic who toured the country ridiculing the Christian faith. They sat together and began talking of religion. Lew Wallace considered himself a Christian, but an unsure one, and his lukewarm faith was no match for Ingersoll's hotheaded, fervent agnosticism. Ingersoll gave him a private two-hour lecture on how silly it was to believe in God or follow the scriptures. You would think it would prove the end of Lew Wallace's feeble faith.

But that interchange lit a fire in Lew Wallace. He would study things for himself and why not write as he studied and continue the story, that began with the wise men's journey and follow it throughout the life of Christ? Wouldn't the necessary research help him to know the answers to Ingersoll's charges against the Christian faith?

And so he wrote, and he studied, and the more he studied, the more convinced he became, until ultimately he found himself, as he described in his own words, "with an absolute belief in God and the Divinity of Christ."

And in the end, he had certainty, and he also had a novel, which he named, "Ben Hur."

"Now the word of the Lord came unto Jonah the son of Amittai, saying, Arise, go to Nineveh, that great city, and cry against it; for their wickedness is come up before me. But Jonah rose up to flee unto Tarshish from the presence of the Lord, and went down to Joppa; and he found a ship going to Tarshish; so he paid the fare thereof, and went down into it, to go with them unto Tarshish from the presence of the Lord." Jonah 1:1-3

Jonah and Me

We've all heard the story of Jonah and the whale, and lots of folks have wondered about it, but did you ever see yourself in the story? We know how it goes, about how God told the prophet Jonah to go to Nineveh with the message that the city would be destroyed if the people didn't repent of their evil ways, and how he didn't want to go to Nineveh and instead took passage on a ship going the opposite direction. Of how God sent a great wind and the resulting storm threatened to capsize the ship, and so the men threw Jonah overboard, hoping to quiet the waves. And the sea grew calm.

It seemed the end of the line for Jonah, but God had prepared a big fish, which swam up and swallowed him whole. After three days and nights, the fish got a stomach ache and vomited him onto dry land. And that's all that most people know. But that is definitely not the end of the story.

First of all, Nineveh was one of the largest cities of the ancient world, the capital city of the kingdom of Assyria. The Assyrians were the enemies of Israel, would ultimately destroy the northern half of the kingdom, and would attempt to defeat the southern half as well. They were a brutal people, known for their cruelty and their heartless ways of dealing with foes. To be captured by the Assyrians was a fate worse than death. It was to this group of people that God wanted Jonah to go, to warn them that they needed to repent or they would be destroyed. But Jonah wouldn't go, didn't want to go, probably actually hoped they would be destroyed!

And here we see the great heart of God, caring not only for His people, the children of Abraham, but all people, even the very wicked of Nineveh. God loved them so much that he sent a prophet to warn them of impending doom. And when the prophet balked, he sent a wind to upset the sea, then a fish to rescue the prophet, and a tummy ache to upset the fish after Jonah had prayed from inside the whale.

Then we see God giving Jonah another chance, another call to go to Nineveh, and this time he went. And he saw the world's biggest revival after giving one of the shortest sermons every preached: "Yet forty days, and Nineveh shall be overthrown." Everyone in the city, from the king on down, dressed in sackcloth and fasted and prayed for mercy, turning from their evil ways and violent lifestyle. And God heard them and spared their city from judgment. But that is still not the end of the story.

In Jonah, chapter four, we find out that Jonah was not so happy with this development. As a matter of fact, he was so angry, he prayed for God to take his life! He couldn't stand it that God had delivered this barbaric city from judgment. And he crawled into a little booth outside the city so he could watch and see what would happen.

And do you know what God did? He caused a plant to quickly grow and give him shade. And then God sent a worm to eat the stem of the plant so that it died, Then he sent a strong east wind, and the sun beat down on Jonah's bare head so he could hardly stand it. And then God talked to Jonah, asking him about why he cared so about his plant and explaining how much he cared about the people of the city.

And the remarkable thing to me is this: God loves a whole city full of people, even wicked people that do horrible things. But he also loves each of us, and works with us patiently when we fall short and fail to respond properly when he calls. Think about it. God called Jonah to Nineveh and he went the other way. So he sent a wind, and a fish, and a tummy ache. Then, when Jonah was back on dry land, he sent Jonah a second time. And when Jonah had his pity party over God's mercy, he sent a plant, and a worm, and an east wind. And then he explained to Jonah his reasoning.

I think Jonah got the message. We have his story in our Bibles, don't we? And I think to myself, if God could use Jonah, a man so full of imperfections, just maybe he can use me.

"A merry heart doeth good like a medicine: but a broken spirit drieth the bones." Proverbs 17:22

Learning to Laugh

Maybe we should call this, "learning to not stop laughing," because young children laugh, studies show, about 400 times a day. Most adults laugh much less often, and many hardly at all. 'Tis a shame; we'd all be healthier and happier if we could continue this childhood habit of laughing: "A merry heart doeth good like a medicine, but a broken spirit drieth the bones," Proverbs 17:22

One of the things I admired so much in my father was his ability to find the humor in tough situations. I remember how, whenever I would meet up with some childhood calamity, such as falling hard on a concrete driveway, he'd respond to my childish tears with concern about the driveway. Do you suppose the driveway is ok? And try to help me laugh through the pain.

It must have been this childhood training that helped me one night when I was grown and had a family of my own. I stranded my family high and dry upon a concrete curbing that I had not seen, which was close to the front door of a busy grocery store. The result was a blown tire, with people pointing and laughing, and I had to laugh also, thinking of the silliness of the whole predicament.

When things go awry, as they often do, it's a great gift if we can find the humor in the situation. For a Christian, especially, who believes that God orders his or her steps (Psalm 37:22), and that ultimately God is in control of every situation (Romans 8:28), and that sometimes even God himself laughs (Psalm 2), why not laugh? It's going to be all right!

Wasn't this the great gift of Ronald Reagan, who could be witty even in tragedy? When he was shot in the spring of 1981 and was met by the team of doctors who would be attempting to save his life, do you know what he said? "Please tell me you are all Republicans!" And how about the reply of the quick-thinking doctor? "We are today!"

Or how about Winston Churchill, who could laugh at himself as well as anybody. He defined success this way: "to be able to go from failure to failure without losing your enthusiasm." He could even turn an attempted correction into a chuckle. Once an aide sent back a piece of his writing because Churchill had ended a sentence with a preposition. Churchill wrote back, "This is the sort of pedantic nonsense up with which I shall not put!"

So when life gets you down, take a deep breath, utter a prayer, giving the situation to God, and laugh a little. It will all work out!

"The Lord give mercy unto the house of Onesiphorus; for he oft refreshed me, and was not ashamed of my chain:" II Timothy 1:16

What's In Your Pockets

Is anything harder to bear than criticism? Especially undeserved criticism? I bet old Abe Lincoln never had to deal with such! Of course not, unless you count his appearance ("Ape Lincoln")' His background ("Country Hick"). His setting slaves free ("tyrant"). His family life, (his wife suffered from mental illness and his young son died while he was president). His leading of the war effort (will it never end?)

Isn't it curious, that when President Abraham Lincoln's pockets were searched on that Good Friday night in April after he had been shot, among his personal items were found press clippings? These clippings made reference to the president: one defending him against charges that his Emancipation Proclamation wasn't strong enough, and another applauding his practical wisdom and faithfulness to the Constitution, and declaring confidence in him as our leader during that dreadful war.

Why do you suppose such writings would be carried on his person, this president so beloved, so universally admired? After all, the man's face is on every penny and his image is carved in great relief at Mt. Rushmore! Could it be that he was not always so appreciated?

Did you know that when he was first elected, a newspaper from his home area of central Illinois, the *Salem Advocate*, said... "he is no more capable of becoming a statesman, nay even a moderate one, than the braying ass can become a noble lion..." The column went on to describe him with words like these: "weak... wishy-washy ...imbecile...disgusting...(making us) the laughing stock of the world."

And during that first winter, between the election and the inauguration, things got worse for President-elect Lincoln, as seven southern states left the Union, and many in the north recanted their support of him. And the war had not even started yet!

Some say that it was the Emancipation Proclamation, written in September of 1862, that marked his transformation from country bumpkin to statesman, but things were not viewed so at the time. The *Chicago Times*, for example, called it "a criminal wrong, and act of national suicide." This proclamation was so unpopular among the soldiers of the Union that a New York Herald correspondent wrote: "the air is thick with revolution... God knows what will be the consequence, but at present matters look dark indeed..."

In the mid-term elections held in November of 1862, President Lincoln's Republican party suffered a crushing defeat. Then in January 1863, the Proclamation actually went into effect and soldiers deserted by the thousands, thinking the wording too strong. Meanwhile, the abolitionists weren't happy either, thinking the wording too weak and because no slaves were actually freed by the document, as it only concerned slavery in the South, which was no longer part of the Union and thus unaffected, and left the slaves in the border states still enslaved.

And when the Republicans re-nominated him in the summer of 1864, it was with no great enthusiasm. James Bennett wrote in the *New York Herald*: "The politicians have again chosen this Presidential pigmy as their nominee." His prospects for winning a second term appeared dim. The *New York World* reprinted an editorial from the *Richmond Examiner,* which said he would never be re-elected and called him an "obscene ape."

Two developments seemed to turn this tide of dislike: First of all, the Democrats chose as their nominee, General George McClellan, a very unpopular and ineffective military commander, choosing as their platform, "The war is a failure, peace now!" And secondly, the military victories began to roll in. Sherman was marching through Georgia and more victories were occurring in the Shenandoah Valley, and just in time for the November elections, which he won in an electoral landslide.

But the popular vote was much closer. He lost heavily in all the big cities, including New York, where he won only 36,000 votes while his opponent garnered 78,000. He won in Ohio and Pennsylvania, but only by half a percentage point.

It wasn't until he was assassinated just a few months later that President Lincoln became truly beloved by the masses. After he was dead he began to be viewed in a different light and people realized the greatness of this humble public servant.

It is good to be reminded of the words of Winston Churchill:

"It's not the critic who counts, nor the man who points out how the strong man stumbled or where the doer of deeds could have done them better. The credit belongs to the man who is actually in the arena, whose face is marred by dust and sweat and blood, who strives valiantly, who errs and comes short again and again, who spends himself in a worthy cause, who at the best knows in the end the triumph of huge achievement, and who at the worst, if he fails, at least, fails while daring greatly, so that his place shall never be with those cold and timid souls who know neither victory nor defeat."

"That ye may be blameless and harmless, the sons of God, without rebuke, in the midst of a crooked and perverse nation, among who ye shine as lights in the world;"
Philippians 2:15

Making a Difference

How in the world can I touch a life, when so many are hurting in so many places, in ways I can only begin to imagine? Many of those I meet in my daily routine I barely know, and I don't know at all most of the ones I pass each day, so can I reach them? I would love to persuade and inspire, encourage and inform. But what platform do I have?

The first solo sung in our fledgling storefront church was entitled, "Little is Much When Good Is In It," and I would suggest that that is the secret. When God is in it, the smallest touch, a simple word of gratitude, a willingness to lend a helping hand, each of these can carry an impact, as illustrated by a story I heard youth speaker Jay Kessler tell years ago.

Jay said he was addressing a group of young people, and afterwards one of the young women came up to speak with him. He said he noticed a scar on her wrist, and knew right away that at some point in the past she had attempted suicide. He talked with her about it, and asked the reason she had not followed through with a second attempt. His actual words, as I recall, were, "Why didn't you do it?"

And she replied, "Well, I had this youth pastor." And she went on to tell how she had watched this man and his wife. She said that sometimes she would be at church before they arrived, and when they pulled in the parking lot, he would open her car door. And as they walked across the parking lot, they would hold hands. She said that a few times when they thought no one was looking, he would actually steal a kiss. And the young woman looked at Jay Kessler and related, "I had this thought, that not every man was like my Dad." That one thought of that one man and his wife, and the example they set, gave her the courage she needed to face the challenges of her life.

That story reminds me that only heaven will reveal how many lives have been touched down through the centuries by folks like these. No, they weren't speaking to thousands in stadiums; no, they did not have throngs of followers on Twitter or friends on Facebook, no television or radio broadcasts. But they lived out their faith in a consistent way, day by day. And the world was watching, changed, one life at a time.

"When Jesus therefore saw her weeping, and the Jews also weeping which came with her, he groaned in the spirit, and was troubled, And said, Where have ye laid him? They said unto him, Lord, come and see. Jesus wept. Then said the Jews, Behold how he loved him!" John 11:33-36

My First Funeral

I was a fresh young pastor, having served barely three months in that role, when I got my first call from our local funeral home proprieter, John Love. Would I conduct a funeral?

Now you must know that funerals come in all varieties and sizes. This would be a graveside service, short in length, and the crowd would be small. The deceased was a woman named Margaret, whom I had never met. She had one surviving relative, a woman named Marilyn. Margaret had been living in Columbus for a number of years, so chances were that few of the local folks would be attending.

The morning of the funeral dawned cold and clear, somewhere in the neighborhood of 10 degrees, as I recall. As predicted, the crowd was indeed small, consisting of one friend named Bea from Columbus, and the sister, Marilyn. Perhaps a few others were there, but not more than two or three. A small blue crowd and a cold green preacher.

Now what do you say at a funeral when you do not know the person who died? I did the best I could to honor her memory, after learning a bit from her sister, and tried to briefly comfort the bereaved (did I mention that it was cold?), speaking of the faithfulness of God and how he is there for us if we will call out to him.

After the service I spoke with Bea, the friend from Columbus, and she told me Margaret had become a Christian and had been growing in her faith throughout her illness. And then she said something that cut me to the core. She said, "I had hoped you would tell them how they, too, could be saved; how they, too, could know Jesus as their Savior."

Well, what could I say? I actually don't remember what I said. But I do know this, it makes all the difference in the world when a person dies, if they die "in the Lord." Were they a Christian? The Bible says in II Corinthians 5:8 that when a Christian dies, they go immediately in to the presence of God! I Thessalonians 5:13-18 speaks of seeing them again as we enjoy an eternal reunion in heaven. Psalm 16:11 describes our loved ones in heaven not resting in peace, but rather celebrating with joy the eternal presence of God.

And so I don't remember what I said to Bea, but I do remember what I said to God. I said, "Please forgive me, Father, for neglecting to share the Gospel. After all, that is the most wonderful news that a person can hear, how if they will turn from their sin and self-righteousness and dare to believe that old gospel message that Jesus died for each of us and rose again the third day, and if they will only call out to him, he will come into that person's heart and change their life!

And I did something else; I made God a promise that I would never again conduct a funeral without telling people how they could become a Christian. And that is a promise I have kept over these last 30-plus years and scores of funeral services.

I also thought I would try to follow up and talk to the surviving sister, Marilyn, but somehow I got busy with other matters and never seemed to find the right time to call on her.

But then about ten years later I heard from some friends that Marilyn was sick and in a long-term care facility. She had cancer and was not expected to survive. And so I went to see her and got reacquainted. Week after week, I would call on her and we would visit. She would tell me what was happening in her life and we would always take time to pray together. But I was troubled for her soul. So one day as we visited together I asked her, "Marilyn, have you ever asked Jesus into your heart?" She replied, "Not before today!" And I knew she was ready to put her faith and trust in the only One that can see us through from life into the next, the Lord Jesus Christ. And so she did.

Now we had another small, short, cold funeral service. But what a difference this time! And I was able to tell Marilyn's story, of how she had found faith in Christ, and perhaps one of those listening would later begin their own faith journey, as they, too, invited the Savior in.

"Therefore whosoever heareth these sayings of mine, and doeth them, I will liken him unto a wise man, which built his house upon a rock: And the rain descended, and the floods came, and the winds blew, and beat upon that house; and it fell not: for it was founded upon a rock. And everyone that heareth these sayings of mine, and doeth them not, shall be likened unto a foolish man, which built his house upon the sand: And the rain descended, and the floods came, and the winds blew, and beat upon that house; and it fell: and great was the fall of it." Matthew 7:24-27

The National Anthem

Is the flag still there? How would you like that for a national anthem title? But that is the question asked in the "Star Spangled Banner." The poem, which was later set to music, was written by a devout Christian named Francis Scott Key, as he anxiously waited for the morning light to discover if Fort McHenry had withstood the bombardment from the British which had lasted throughout the night.

Why the concern? Because the flag was the great indicator of whether or not we were still in possession of the fort and of Baltimore harbor. But the flag meant more than that. It was a symbol of the "land of the free and the home of the brave." All the honor and ideals of our new nation, as Abraham Lincoln later said so well, "conceived in liberty and dedicated to the proposition that all men are created equal," were rolled into that one piece of cloth, our flag.

I wonder if Mr. Key realized that the battle for our nation would continue long after the War of 1812, that the precepts and great truths that our nation was built upon would continue to be attacked. Sometimes the danger has been as obvious missiles in the night, but at other times the enemies of our republic have chosen more subtle weapons, and have attempted to wear away our resolve through propaganda and deceit.

Yes, the flag is still there. But so is the conflict. And just as surely as good soldiers were in short supply then, so is it now. Think of the great ideals of our nation: individual liberty, freedom of speech and religion, hatred of tyranny. But the foundation that these principles rest upon is the reliability and authority of the scriptures and the applied teaching of the Word of God, which tells me of the importance of family, how to tell right from wrong, of the necessity of sacrifice, that we aren't here by accident, that we all will give account to Almighty God for what we've done with this liberty of ours. Our Lord Jesus said that a house built on his applied teaching was a house built on the rock, and that a house built on anything else was a house built on sand! Matthew 7:24-27.

It has been said that the price of liberty is eternal vigilance. Can we be ever watchful, not just for the flag that flies so high, but for the foundation our nation rests upon?

Don't we owe this to those who have gone before, many of whom paid the ultimate price to give us this freedom we so enjoy? For some, it will mean more time at home, for others, more reaching into the lives of those who are hurting. For all of us, it means becoming aware of the battles in our world, and to be willing to speak up, to pray, to encourage, to vote.

May God help us to be faithful. It's our turn.

"Through God we shall do valiantly: for he it is that shall tread down our enemies." Psalm 60:12

Poor George

He had ambitions to be somebody, to do something with his life. But what a beginning! Born to a new mother with a newly widowed father who already had a family of four children from his first marriage, his early days must have been hard. Their house was small, and the children slept in the attic, taking care not to bump their heads on the rafters. He was the oldest child of the second set of children; five more would come after him.

Poor George – He might have amounted to something notable, but his father died when George was just eleven, and he left home to live with his half-brother so he could attend school a little longer. Even so, his education ended when he was 14, and he was working full time at age 16. That he never got a college education was a lifelong regret.

Poor George - He had had a chance to go to sea, which had been the launching of many a young man into fame and fortune, and a chance to see the world. But his mother stood in the way. She seemed to enjoy this sort of thing, was good at frustrating him throughout his entire life, never seeming to enjoy the accomplishments he did achieve, never indicating the slightest pride in the man he became.

Poor George - Maybe if his health had been better...but malaria and small pox took their toll, along with the lifestyle he adopted which included constant travel and privation, exposure to the elements, and worse. How he survived at all is a wonder. If only he had been born at a different time in history.

And then, as if to make the odds against success even greater, he took sides in that great conflict that swept across our land, that would pit neighbor against neighbor, friend against friend, even father (or mother) against son. And what's worse, he took the weaker side, choosing to serve in an army that had little organization, irregular pay, where many would die from exposure and malnutrition. And the enemy was so much better equipped, so much better trained.

And if that weren't enough, he agreed to be a leader, a general, in this rag tag army, even though he really felt unqualified. He hadn't trained at West Point, knew next to nothing about the great battles of history and the strategies of Napoleon or Julius Caesar.

But he did have a way of getting away from the enemy with his army still intact, of surviving to fight another day. And every now and then, Poor George showed a flash of brilliance, and this brilliance, mixed with a great deal of courage, and much dependence on and appreciation for Divine intervention, plus his way of winning the love and devotion of the men serving under him, would see him through to the end of the fighting.

And so we don't think of him today as Poor George, the man who might have been. We think of him as a man who dared great things, who didn't let the obstacles of his life hold him back. We think of him as the father of our country, George Washington.

"Give, and it shall be given unto you; good measure, pressed down, and shaken together, and running over, shall men give into your bosom. For with the same measure that ye mete withal it shall be measured to you again." Luke 6:38

A Roadside Parable

This story is loosely based on one I heard many years ago, from whom or by whom I have no recollection.

Aatish sat quietly in the dust of the roadside, just another beggar along the crowded streets of Delhi. As each person approached, he felt the same hopeful surging – maybe this one would stop and notice him, maybe give a few grains of rice, or perhaps even a coin or two? This didn't happen very often, but at least once a week he would receive something more, enough for him to buy a bit of meat that tasted so delicious and actually quieted the hunger in his belly for a few hours.

The years had rolled along, and each day was the same. The crowds, the yelling, the filth and the smell, the indifference of most who walked along, and what was hardest of all to bear, the sneer of those who looked at Aatish as if he were vermin. Indifference was easier to bear than the disgust communicated by those who had never faced misfortune, who had never lost their position, who had never been forced to beg.

But he was thankful for the few who had compassion, who took a moment to stop and not only look kindly on him, and even, along with their alms, gave a word of greeting and encouragement. They actually treated him like .... a human being.

And today had been a good day; no coins, but a quite a bit of rice, and soon his cup would be half full! Why, cook that with some water, and maybe a locust or two, which he might catch if he were quick enough, and he could survive another night on the street!

The shadows of the day began to deepen, and Aatish began to think of finding a good place to rest for the evening, when a strange excitement swept through the crowded street. The rajah was coming! The rajah was coming! Oh, this had never been, not in this part of Delhi! He was approaching on foot, along with his entourage of footmen who tended to his every need. Wouldn't it be something if the rajah would stop at his cup!

Slowly he made his way up the street. It seemed to take forever before he came clearly into view. The rajah looked around, at the vendors, the craftsmen and women, and yes, even at the beggars. And yes, he even looked at Aatish. What it was about him that caught his eye, he would never know, but the rajah approached Aatish. Would he give him a coin? Maybe even a silver coin? Maybe even a gold one? Who knew what might happen?

The rajah stopped and looked at Aatish; he held out his cup hopefully. The rajah looked into the cup. And he held out his hand and said, "Give me your rice!" Aatish could not believe his ears! This was not the way it was supposed to be! Instinctively, he pulled back his arm. No!

This was his rice! What did the rajah need with his rice? No!

But the rajah didn't go away. Instead, his eyes held steady on the beggar and he repeated his request. "Give me your rice!" And in that day, a beggar dared not refuse a rajah, so Aatish reached in o his cup and took out three grains and placed them in the hand of the rajah. Maybe that would satisfy him? Maybe now he would go away?

But the rajah didn't go away. Instead he reached for the silk bag hanging at his waist. He opened the bag and took out three diamonds and placed them in the cup of Aatish. And Aatish began to weep, not because suddenly he was a wealthy man, but he wept because he realized what might have been, if only he had given him more.

"Blessed (happy) is the man that walketh not in the counsel of the ungodly, nor standeth in the way of sinners, nor sitteth in the seat of the scornful. But his delight is in the law of the Lord, and in his law doth he meditate day and night. And he shall be like a tree planted by the rivers of water, that bringeth forth his fruit in his season; his leaf also shall not wither; and whatsoever he doeth shall prosper." Psalm 1:1-3

Sparky Was a Loser

"Sparky Was a Loser." The title caught my eye; it was one of the stories in a compiling of Paul Harvey broadcasts. And when I think of Paul Harvey, I think of my father and remember fondly the times we sat in his fuel oil truck and listened to his noon broadcast while we ate our lunch.

In the afternoon, Paul Harvey had another daily broadcast, this one only lasting five minutes or so. It was called the "Rest of the Story," and featured some little known facet of a well-known celebrity or historical figure, whose identity was often kept secret till the very end.

This story about Sparky was one of the stories featured on this shorter broadcast. It was the story of a young man who early on in life felt very much a misfit, who constantly tried and failed in many areas: at sports, at romance, in academics, at life itself.

But according to Paul Harvey, the one thing Sparky could do was draw, not serious art, but rather, cartoon characters. He had an idea of a comic strip featuring the trials and tribulations of a young boy facing constant failure. And as he tried to convince publishers of the merits of this strip, he faced more and more rejection. But one day a national cartoon syndicate agreed to give him a try. And so "Peanuts" made its debut in 1952, appearing in the grand total of seven newspapers.

The "hook" of this "Rest of the Story" story was that Charlie Brown was really Sparky, whose real name was Charles Shulz. And as you probably already know, Charles Shulz would go on to become the most successful cartoonist in history—the most influential, the most popular, the richest. And Charlie Brown's dog, Snoopy, would become known around the world, one of the most recognizable characters of all time.

And we're not just talking comic strips. Charles Shulz would go on to greater success with best-selling books, a Christmas special that is still a great favorite, a play that would become the most produced musical production ever, called, "Your a Good Man, Charlie Brown." No one thought of Sparky as a loser now.

But now it's time for our own, "Rest of the Story."

In 1952, when Peanuts began running daily in papers across America, Charles Shulz was a newly-married man, a strong Christian known for his church involvement and his faith in Christ, glad to adopt a little girl from his wife's first marriage, and together they would have four more children. They would soon leave their native Minnesota and move to California, the land of wide open spaces and opportunity.

But a funny thing happened on the way to success. Although more and more doors opened for him, he was unable to shake the feeling of being a failure, of being unhappy. And he also felt that somehow the inspiration for the ongoing trials of Charlie Brown required his own ongoing sadness, and so he refused counseling or psychological help of any kind.

As the years rolled along, he became more and more devoted to his work, even to the point of considering the children of his cartoon strip to be his second family. One revealing interview (overheard by his daughter and related by her) gives us a peak into his heart. He was asked, "How are your kids?" And he began talking about the Peanuts cast. And the interviewer said, "No, Sparky, how are your five kids?" And his daughter added, "Were we his everything? No. His strip was his everything."

And with so much attention paid to so many projects, less and less was paid to his wife, and they began to grow apart. Ultimately this great family man got involved with a woman more than twenty years younger. When his wife found out, he promised to stop the affair, but he did not even proposing marriage while still married. After this affair ended, he soon was involved again with another, this time marrying the woman after divorcing his wife

Looking back at the cartoons drawn during this period of his life, hints were given about what was going on behind the scenes. Crabby, bossy Lucy was understood to be representative of his wife, the one who always jerked the football away before he could kick it. And the little red-headed girl that Charlie Brown couldn't get over was really a red-head that left Charles Shulz hurting for a lifetime.

And somewhere along the way, Charles Shulz, the strong outspoken Christian, lost his faith. In later years someone called him a secular humanist, and he didn't disagree. He and his second wife bought a home together, and on the grounds was a chapel which they used for the wedding ceremony. Then they turned it into a gym.

At the age of 77 his health began to fail and he was diagnosed with stage 4 colon cancer. On his deathbed, one friend observed, "He was angry – angry at God, angry with friends, angry with fate. He did not accept death gracefully – he wasn't ready."

A few years earlier, as Charles Shulz had approached his seventy-fifth birthday, he reflected on his life and what it all meant. And he said, in summing up, "What a waste."

Maybe Paul Harvey had it right after all, Sparky was a loser. But now, to revisit another Paul Harvey phrase, wash your ears out with this:

Along about the same time as Charles Shulz was growing up in a city in the north, another boy was growing up in a city in the south. He was called "Lightning" for a nickname, at least for a while, so we'll call him that also.

Looking at young Lightning, would you say he

was destined to be a winner or a loser? See him now at age 6, riding his bike to a bar, pleading with his father to come home? See the father resisting, resisting, then finally relenting, staggering from the bar, throwing the bike in the back seat and driving them both home?

See Lightning at age 10, waiting with his friends for the church bells to toll, signaling time for services to start. He's waiting, not for church, but for the men gathered outside the church for one last smoke, to toss to the ground their half-smoked cigarettes and cigars. Now they all had smokes for the day!

See Lightning at age 12, running the streets, unsupervised, one by one his friends disappearing, then reappearing in reform school. It seemed only a matter of time until he would join them there. Lightning seemed destined to be a loser, for sure.

But seeing these developments greatly concerned his mother and father, and so they moved out of the inner city, out to the rural suburbs, where Lightning could be more closely supervised and given productive work to do. One job led to another as all that energy was harnessed.

Another change occurred about that same time, as he began, along with his family, to attend church. Not long after, he went forward in that little church to ask Jesus into his heart and a short while later, both he and his father were baptized in the river flowing through their town. Church became a vital part of his life. Lightning was forming new friendships and new habits.

By the age of 17, Lightning considered himself an adult. He quit school, not so he could loaf his way through life, but so he could work full time. He got a job driving a dump truck and became known for his industry, for being first to load in the morning and squeezing more trips into the hours of a workday than any other driver. You wouldn't equate his name with "loser" now.

And then he saw a girl, saw her working in front of a store, and stopped to meet her. She didn't want to have anything to do with him, said she didn't know him. So he introduced himself. They went on a date, then another. On the second date, he proposed. She thought he was just a kid who didn't really know what he wanted, but he wasn't, and he did. Less than a year later they were married; he was 18.

And so the story goes. The two of them built a life together. Raised a family, four children who thought the world of them both. Built a business. Stayed married, stayed in church, kept the faith. Faithfully lived out in their actions what they believed in their hearts. Never became rich or famous, but both of them were surely happy with the life they had together.

But the story doesn't end there. He kept working, not retiring completely until age 85, when his wife's failing memory and loss of vision meant he needed to stay home, taking care of her needs without complaint. And after 70 years of marriage, Sunday mornings would still find them in church, still holding hands.

And the rest is history. He stayed true to her until death, then followed her a year and a half later. His passing made no headlines; he left no vast estate for his heirs to fight over. But Lightning surely was a winner. I should know. I am his son.

*"Then shall the righteous answer him, saying,
Lord, when saw we thee an hungred, and fed thee? Or
thirsty, and gave thee drink? When saw we thee a
stranger, and took thee in? or naked, and clothed thee?
Or when saw we thee sick, or in prison, and came unto
thee? And the King shall answer and say unto them, Verily I say unto you, inasmuch as ye have done it unto one of
the least of these my brethren, ye have done it unto me."*
Matthew 25:37-40

Surprised in That Day

In 1872 a young preacher named DL Moody
heard British evangelist Henry Varley say something that
was to change his life: "It remains for the world to see
what the Lord can do with a man wholly consecrated to
Christ." And Moody responded within his heart, "I resolve to be that man."

Moody had already experienced more success in
his brief twelve years of ministry than most could ever
dream. His Sunday School in Chicago had grown to
1,500 in attendance. He served the boys in blue with
great distinction during the Civil War, and in 1865 was
elected president of the YMCA, injecting new life in that
organization.

But the statement made by Varley challenged him
greatly. Though very poorly educated himself, he gave

himself to the cause of Christian education, founding the Northfield Seminary for girls, The Mount Hermon School for boys, both in Massachusetts, and a school in Chicago that would become the Moody Bible Institute, whose thousands of graduates would go on to serve Christ around the world.

Meanwhile, he was not neglecting his gift of evangelism. He teamed with musician and song leader Ira Sankey, preaching first in 1873 to crowds in England, then Scotland and Ireland and especially America. Over the next 26 years he traveled a million miles, preached to 100 million people, and 750,000 became Christians after hearing him give the old time gospel message of new life in Jesus Christ.

In later years, someone spoke with Henry Varley about what he said to Moody, and how God had used those words to light a fire under Moody, to stir him to serve with a new passion. And Varley said he did not remember making that statement.

In Matthew 25, our Lord Jesus said there would be some surprised folks at the time of judgment, folks who had no memory of special service to our Lord. But Jesus said, "in as much as you have done it unto one of the least of these my brethren, you have done it unto me."

It seems to me that people aren't necessarily impacted so much by our well-thought-out words and prepared programs and procedures, but by the simple truths spoken by sincere hearts, by the silent sermon of a consistent life, trying to live the way Jesus taught. These lives are marked by compassion and concern, faithfulness and love, secret prayer.

It just may be that your life has made more of a difference than you know. But you will know in that day, for the Lord is always faithful, and He remembers even when we forget.

"For God is not unjust to forget your work and labor of love which you have shown toward His name, in that you have ministered to the saints, and do minister."

Hebrews 6:10

"But none of these things move me, neither count I my life dear unto myself, so that I might finish my course with joy, and the ministry, which I received of the Lord Jesus, to testify the gospel of the grace of God." Acts 20:24

Churchill's Secret

He had the face of a bulldog. Or so it's always appeared to me. And I'm told that the bulldog was bred with massive jaws for one purpose, to clamp down on the nose of an unruly bull and hold on. That's what we call this combination of courage and determination, tenacity.

And when British Prime Minister Winston Churchill had a chance to speak to the boys at the school he had attended as a young man, many were surprised at the brevity of his remarks. He made a few general comments, then got right to the heart of the matter. He said, "Never give in. Never give in. Never, never, never, never – in nothing great or small, large or petty – never give in, except to convictions of honor and good sense." And then he sat down.

When he spoke those words in the fall of 1941, surely everyone assumed he was once again trying to rally the spirits of the British people to fight on against Hitler's Nazi Germany, even though the odds were surely not in their favor. And no doubt, that was his aim. But perhaps it was more than that. Perhaps he was giving a glimpse of the secret of his success.

Some would give a quick glance at his background, and say, "What's the big deal? He was born to the aristocracy, into a rich and successful family. His father had achieved great heights in politics and surely paved the way for his only son.

But did you know that he certainly had no easy childhood? Born prematurely, he was often sick and had the great misfortune of being accident-prone. To his busy and successful parents, he was largely viewed as a nuisance and was raised mostly by his nanny before being sent off to boarding school at the age of eight.

At school he was bullied by the other boys and beaten by the teachers whenever he broke one of the rules, of which there were many. Academically, he did well with subjects like history, but struggled with Latin and math, which were considered more important. His teachers certainly saw no greatness in his future.

It was thought perhaps that military school would be the place for him, but he failed the entrance exam, so he took it again, and failed again, and finally passed on the third try. He did well in the military, fighting in India and the Sudan.

He came home and ran for a seat in Parliament, and was defeated. His next stop was to serve as a newspaper correspondent covering the Boer War in South Africa. He was captured, but managed to escape, traveling over hundreds of miles of wilderness before rejoining the army and fighting so heroically he was nominated for the Victorian Cross. He came home, ran for Parliament again, this time succeeding.

When World War I came along, he had been given the post of First Lord of the Admiralty and was considered a brilliant tactician. He conceived a daring plan that, if executed properly, would have saved the lives of thousands of British soldiers. But it was poorly executed, and thousands were slaughtered on the beaches of Gallipoli. The blame was placed on him, and he had to resign his office and ended up in the trenches, fighting in France until his name was cleared. He was back in the cabinet when the war ended.

On a personal level, he was very happily married to his wife, Clementine, and loved their life together with their children. But the death of his little girl, Marigold, at age three, was almost too much to bear. And then there were his legendary bouts of depression...

Financially, he was a very wealthy man, until the stock market crashed in 1929 and took most of his fortune. Then he was hit by a car in New York City and nearly died.

Along about this time, a young politician began to rise in popularity in Germany by the name of Adolph Hitler. He was re-arming Germany in violation of the peace treaty signed at the end of the first world war and almost no one seemed to notice, no one, that is, except Churchill. He began to openly oppose his nation's appeasement of the coming tyrant and became a laughing-stock to many, a fear-monger to others, and a general nuisance to those in power who truly detested the man.

But when Hitler's true colors were revealed, the

people of England realized that Churchill had been right all along, and he became Prime Minister, the one who would rally the people of England to fight on, even when it seemed hopeless, when England stood alone against the man who had conquered the whole of the European continent.

By the time of Churchill's speech, the Soviet Union had entered the war against Germany, and within six weeks, the United States would also take up the cause after the bombing of our naval base at Pearl Harbor. The tide was truly turning! And the allied forces would go on to defeat Germany in the spring of 1945.

But why was this one man, Winston Churchill, so singularly used to change the tide of history? Perhaps the answer was revealed in the brief speech given at his childhood school; he simply didn't know when to quit.

"Verily, verily, I say unto you, He that heareth my word, and believeth on him that sent me, hath everlasting life, and shall not come into condemnation; but is passed from death unto life." John 5:24

The Charles Ruth Story

What does it take for a man or woman to be effective for Christ? Superior talent? A head full of knowledge? Let me relate to you a story I heard a number of years ago which challenged me greatly.

It was the summer of 1975. I had just finished my freshman year of Bible college in Chattanooga, Tennessee and I had two jobs. During the week I worked at the Christian camp affiliated with my school, and on weekends I traveled with a gospel singer, Marvin Harris, as his pianist.

Those weekends that summer would find us traveling to various churches throughout the south, but one Sunday Marvin had a booking in a small town in Pennsylvania, some 700 miles away. Most of the churches we visited have left my memory, but for some reason several events stand out in my mind from that weekend. For instance, I remember getting a haircut while there, memorable because in those days I had a lot of hair, but that barber must have seen in me a mission project. I still remember how Marvin laughed when I returned from my "scalping,"

And I remember the violin solo that a young woman played that night, with only three strings, and those out of tune. To this day, it was the worst solo I ever heard in any church at any time.

And I remember how after Marvin's concert on Sunday evening, when we were ready to leave for our all-night drive back to Tennessee, the church treasurer was not to be found, and he was the one with our love offering, from which our expenses would be paid. Now for me, as a young single man with few bills, this was not a big deal. But Marvin had a family to support, so. while we couldn't find the treasurer, we did find his car Marvin parked his car in front of his, blocking his escaping with our funds whenever he returned from wherever he had gone (for ice cream in another town we were told).

And I remember that, when the man did finally return and gave us our check, it was barely enough to pay for our gas for the 1,400 mile round trip.

But let me tell you the best part of the weekend. This is the story I was going to tell you earlier.

An old man approached me that Sunday and told me about a man he once knew named Charles Ruth. Charles had lived in a certain town in New Jersey and had become a Christian later in life, had lived a rather rough life, and thus knew many of the local "down-and-outers." He had a passion for these men to come to know the Christ that had so changed his life, and so he set out to talk to them about their souls.

This old man said that Charles Ruth's method was very simple. He would read to them one verse from the Bible, John 5:24. And then Mr. Ruth would explain how a person could personally put their faith and trust in Jesus Christ. And the old man said that in the years this man had left, he led more men to Christ than all the preachers in that New Jersey town put together, and there were twelve of them.

After hearing this story, I was moved that such a simple method could produce such an effect. And the old man said, "And that's not all! When he died, he requested that his body be arranged in his coffin with an open Bible and his finger pointed to the words of John 5:24."

A large crowd came to the funeral home to honor him, especially the homeless for whom he had cared deeply. And many of those who had resisted his appeals to trust in Christ, found their hearts softened as they read again the words of John 5:24, and knelt at his casket and trusted Christ.

And the old man continued, "And that's not all!" And he explained how that on his tombstone along with his name and date of birth and death, were the words of John 5:24.

"Verily, verily, I say unto you, He that heareth my word, and believeth on him that sent me, hath everlasting life, and shall not come into condemnation, but is passed from death unto life."

"Why art thou cast down, O my soul? And why art thou disquieted within me? Hope thou in God: for I shall yet praise him, who is the health of my countenance, and my God." Psalm 42:11

The Lesson of Elijah

He thought it was the end. The queen was after him, had threatened his life, and so he ran, ran, and ran some more, until he was miles into the wilderness. And there, spent and alone, he poured out his heart to God and prayed to die. "It is enough! Now, Lord, take my life!" Read it for yourself in the book of I Kings, chapter 19.

He thought he was the only believer left in Israel. The entire nation seemed hopelessly entrapped in idolatry, until that great showdown with the 400 prophets of Baal on top of Mount Carmel. It had seemed a great victory when the thousands of his countrymen had gone from utter silence when challenged with whether to follow Baal or Jehovah God, to everyone falling on their faces and saying, "The Lord, He is God! The Lord, He is God!" But the victory was only temporary, as getting idols out of hearts would prove much harder than eliminating their prophets. And Queen Jezebel had sent him a threatening message, "So let the gods do to me, and more also, if I do not make your life as the life of one of them by tomor-

101

row..."

Surely God was through with him! And he lay down, exhausted physically from his run, exhausted emotionally and spiritually from his battles with Ahab & Jezebel and trying so hard to be God's man in a hostile time, and he slept.

Now, while Elijah sleeps, let us think about his case.

He thought he was the only believer in God left in Israel. He says twice in this chapter, "I alone am left; and they seek to take my life." But the Lord answers and tells him of 7,000 others who have not bowed their knees to Baal.

He thought it was the end. But the chapter ends with new orders for Elijah, as he tells him of new men to anoint as kings of Israel and Syria, and of a new prophet named Elisha that would assist him and ultimately succeed him as God's man for Israel.

And how would God deal with this depressed prophet now sleeping? Well, He dealt tenderly with him, providing food and water and direction for the future. He had thought he was alone in the wilderness, but he learned anew the lesson David shared from Psalm 139, "Where can I go from your Spirit? Or where can I flee from your presence? If I take the wings of the morning, and dwell in the uttermost parts of the sea, even there your hand shall lead me, and your right hand shall hold me."

And so Elijah awoke, went on to anoint those chosen by God and to finish his work on earth. And in a fitting finish to a great life and ministry well lived, he was taken to heaven in a whirlwind, with chariot and horses of fire. II Kings 2.

Let us learn the lesson of Elijah. Depression is not the unpardonable sin. Even great men and women of God have suffered with it. But keep the faith. It's not over until God says it's over. Your best days may well be yet to come. And know this, you are never alone, for Jesus has said, "I will never leave you nor forsake you." Hebrews 13:5.

"Hearken unto thy father that begat thee, and despise not thy mother when she is old." Proverbs 23:22

The Old Man

He sits alone in his favorite chair, trying to pass the time. In other years he was so busy with life that he hardly had time to sit. But now all he has is time. And all he can do is sit.

He sits alone in his favorite chair, but not really alone, for he still has his memories of days gone by. And he's thankful, because many his age don't even have that. He likes to remember his wife of so many years and all the good times they had, and their babies that grew so fast and now are grown and busy with families of their own.

He sits alone in his favorite chair, but not really alone, for he's surrounded by the prayers and thoughts of family and friends who haven't forgotten he's there. And even now as winter approaches, they study hard on what to buy the old man for Christmas.

They used to ask, "What do you buy for a man who has everything?" Now they ask, "What do you buy for a man who has nothing?" He needs no clothes, he has no car, and he can't see to read anything you'd bring.

But what he would appreciate the most is a little time with you. The one thing that would really put a smile on his face would be to see a smile on your face, as you come down the hall for a visit.

"If ye know these things, happy are ye if you do them." John 13:17

The Quiet Man

When I entered college as a freshman in the fall of 1974, I auditioned for a part in a traveling college singing ensemble. I didn't make the team. I also auditioned for the school play, and was delighted to learn I had been given one of the larger roles. So the following year, when play time rolled around, I again tried out, this time rather confidently. The director of that play was the same as the first, and since we seemed to get along well, I assumed I would be given a choice part.

My confidence was so great that I persuaded my friend, Rob, to audition as well. I even told him I would put in a good word for him with the director. Imagine my chagrin when the parts were assigned. He was given a leading role. I was given a few lines, assigned a character with no name, and what few lines I had were to be spoken on a darkened stage, behind a scrim, like a character in a shadow-play. After the production ended and the cast lined up to be greeted by our audience, I was asked by some who knew me, "were you in the play?" I was not by any measure the star!

Now, what if I were to tell you about a Bible character who played a major role in that first Christmas story, yet had no lines. Indeed, we read about what he thought, and about what he did, but not one word of his is recorded. There is no doubt that he spoke, that he was a person of great influence, but nothing he said was written for us by which we could remember him. Someone has called him the "forgotten man of the manger." I am referring of course, to Joseph, the husband of Mary, the man chosen of God to marry the virgin Mary and to raise our Lord Jesus.

All we know of him is recorded for us in the first chapters of the gospels of Matthew and Luke. Matthew 1 tells us that Mary was espoused to him, and an angel appeared to him and explained that the baby she was carrying was the Son of God, and that he was to go ahead and take her as his wife. And he did.

The next chapter tells of another angelic visit, this time warning him to flee with his young family to Egypt. And he did. And after the death of King Herod, again an angel appeared to him and told him to return to Israel. And he did. And one more time he was given divine direction, this time told to settle in the area of Galilee. And he did.

That's basically it. Four times given direction from God. And four times he obeyed. And from all appearances, it seems he was a good earthly father to our Lord Jesus, teaching him his trade of carpentry.

What is success? Can it be measured in dollars? Position? Fame? Pleasures or experiences? When it comes our time to stand before our Lord and give account of our lives, as the Bible tells us we each will do, can anything better be said of us than this? That we learned what we were to do. And we did it.

"Who can find a virtuous woman? For her price is far above rubies. The heart of her husband doth safely trust in her, so that he shall have no need of spoil. Her children arise up and call her blessed; her husband also, and he praiseth her." Proverbs 31:10,11,28

The Woman Who Stayed

Sally felt a fool. Married the old boyfriend. Swallowed his line about being a prosperous farmer. Believed him when he spoke of the home he owned in a neighboring state. I mean, after all, he was wearing a nice suit and had on a new pair of boots! He spoke of prosperity and servants! It seemed too good to be true!

Sally had had her share of grief. Single mother of three, left a widow by a man with no business sense but a great deal of debt. She and the first husband had struggled from the start, with his being already behind on his taxes the very first year of their marriage. How could things get any worse? Then he died, and since their home had been included as part of his job as the county jailer, when he died they had to scramble to find another place to live. A widow at age 27, and three young children.

So when after three years of struggling to survive, old boyfriend Tom, who was now a widower with two children of his own, came a-calling and proposed marriage immediately, the whole thing seemed a godsend! And when I say immediately, I mean immediately. When he knocked and she answered, he said, basically, "Hello Sally! So good to see you after all these years! How about getting married?" And since she was a desperate woman in a desperate situation, she agreed on one condition. He needed to settle the debts left by her late husband. And so the debts were paid, the marriage was performed, the wagon was loaded and off they went to begin their new life together.

Now you have to understand that these were primitive times. But primitive or not, what she found upon their arrival at the new home was upsetting. The small log cabin was really more of a hut, with no windows to be found and a dirt floor besides. And they were supposed to live there, with their combined family of seven, plus a young cousin he had taken in? And the prosperous farm was nothing of the sort, covered in blackberry thorns and sumac bushes. And servants? Don't make me laugh! In today's terms, you would say she'd been had.

Her first instinct was to leave. This was not what she had in mind when Tom spoke of the joyful adventure of their new life together. But what to do? And as she weighed her options, and no doubt prayed for guidance, her eyes fell on the ten-year-old boy that was now her step-son. There was something about the way he looked at her that convinced her that here was more than just a boy; here was a kindred spirit. And she said, "I will stay for the sake of this boy." And she did.

And she did more than stay. She helped him, encouraged him, saw the value in his mind and in his soul. And when his father carried on about how learning was a waste of time, she stood by him and his ambition to be more than what he was. She loved him; believed in him.

In later years, when men everywhere reverenced his name, they would wonder about this woman he spoke so kindly of, the woman of whom he said, "All that I am or ever hope to be, I owe to my angel mother." She was the woman who could have walked away, but didn't. She was the woman who stayed for the sake of a ten year old boy with a certain look in his eye, named Abraham, Abraham Lincoln.

"And he was in the hinder part of the ship, asleep on a pillow: and they awake him, and say unto him, Master, carest thou not that we perish? And he arose and rebuked the wind, and said unto the sea, Peace, be still. And the wind ceased, and there was a great calm. And he said unto them, why are ye so fearful? How is it that ye have no faith? And they feared exceedingly, and said one to another, What manner of man is this, that even the wind and the sea obey him?" Mark 4:38-41

Was It a Miracle or Not?

Much has been made of the wonderful success of D-Day, June 6, 1944, when hundreds of thousands of Allied soldiers crossed the English Channel, landing on the beaches of Normandy and beginning the invasion of Europe, ultimately setting that continent free from the bloody grip of the Nazi reign of terror.

But let me tell you about another crossing of the English Channel which occurred four years earlier. This crossing was not an invasion; it was a retreat, an evacuation on a massive scale. If it had not succeeded, the outcome of the Second World War would have almost certainly been very different. England would have lost her army and been forced to settle with Hitler, and all of Europe would have remained under German control.

Dunkirk. Over 300,000 soldiers, most of them British, but also French, Polish, Belgian and Canadian armed forces had been trapped there along the English Channel when the Germans had so breathtakingly roared across France with their Panzer tank divisions and, in only two weeks had reached the coast. The harbors had almost all been destroyed and there was no way to get all but a few of the British warships close enough to retrieve the soldiers. It was hoped that maybe 40,000 could be rescued.

But a funny thing happened on the way to the massacre. Hitler ordered his tanks to stop 8 miles short of Dunkirk, planning to leave the final destruction of the Allied army to the Luftwaffe (German airforce). But a massive storm grounded many of the planes. An appeal had been made to the British boat owners, and some 700 boats were sent or brought over: fishing boats, lifeboats, barges, private craft of all types and sizes. A fog settled in, and the notoriously rough waters of the English Channel were stilled long enough for the small boats to come ashore and rescue those stranded and deliver them to the larger warships waiting offshore to carry them safely back to England, where they were given a hero's welcome home.

Today, some say this was no miracle. A tour guide at Dover Castle, where the invasion was then planned and today houses a display explaining the evacuation, was heard to say, "Some people may call the Dunkirk evacuation a miracle, but I put it down to the organization of Vice Admiral Bertram Ramsay." Two movies about Dunkirk have been released in the last few years, but neither mention the miracle aspect.

But is there another explanation as to why Hitler would suddenly order his tanks to stop just 8 miles from the retreating Allied army? No one today can give a rational explanation. But did you know that the Bible says in Proverbs 21:1 that the king's heart is in God's hand, that he turns it as he pleases.

And can you explain the timing of the storm that grounded the aircraft, and then the fog and quietness of the waters of the English Channel? Have we forgotten how our Lord Jesus calmed the storm on the Sea of Galilee with three simple words, "Peace, be still?"

And did you know that on May 26, 1940, before the evacuation began, the king of England had called for a national day of prayer? This special appeal is not mentioned in the Dover Castle display, but the believers of England flocked to their churches in massive numbers to pray for deliverance.

And what did the people who lived through this great event think? One letter to the editor of the London Times spoke for many, "Surely our prayers have been answered in the merciful deliverance of our Expeditionary Force from complete destruction." Even Prime Minister Winston Churchill considered it a miracle of deliverance.

And did you know that on June 9, 1940, there was a national day of thanksgiving declared for the nation of England? And of this day, the London Telegraph reported, "One thing can be certain about tomorrow's thanksgiving in our churches. From none will the thanks ascend with greater sincerity or deeper fervor than from the officers and men who have seen the hand of God, powerful to save, delivering them from the hands of a mighty foe, who, humanly speaking, had them utterly at his mercy."

We often remind ourselves that we must not forget the bloody price paid for our freedoms by those who have fought and died in our armed forces, but is it not just as important that we not forget all the wonderful answers to prayer, when our Lord came through for us in ways we can't explain to deliver from disaster? "Oh that men would praise the Lord for his goodness, and for his wonderful works to the children of men!" Psalm 107:8

"The ear that heareth the reproof of life abideth

among the wise. He that refuseth instruction despiseth his own soul: but he that heareth reproof getteth understanding. The fear of the Lord is the instruction of wisdom; and before honor is humility."

Proverbs 15:31-33

Why Did Peter Fail

You remember the story. The gospels tell it very well. Jesus and his band of disciples. Troubling developments. Celebrating Passover together. His telling them that this night they would all be offended. The prayer in the garden. The sleepy disciples. The kiss of Judas. The soldiers and the arrest. It was a night to remember in the worst sense of the word.

But in a scene that staggers the mind and breaks the heart, when Jesus is desperately short of friends and while he is being interrogated, a young servant girl accused Peter as he warmed himself by the fire in he courtyard, "You were also with Jesus of Galilee!"

And Peter responded, "I do not know what you are saying!" He went out to the gateway.

Another girl said, "This fellow also was with Jesus of Nazareth."

This time he denied with an oath, "I do not know the Man!"

A little bit later several men came up and said to Peter, "Surely you also are one of them, for your speech betrays you."

Peter began to curse and swear, saying, "I do not know the Man!

And in the distance a rooster crowed.

How could Peter do this? Deny the man he had followed so closely for three years; deny the one who he would identify as the "Christ, the Son of the Living God!"

Well, here's the short answer. When Jesus was arrested and being led away, the disciples scattered, but Peter followed from afar. (Matthew 26:58)

Well, why was he following from afar? Remember the details of that night? The conversations and interactions? Remember what Jesus had to say to Peter?

"If I wash you not, you have no part with me." This, in response to Peter's telling Jesus that he would not wash his feet.

"You will deny me 3 times before the rooster crows." This, in response to Peter's profession of loyalty.

"Could you not watch with me one hour?" This in response to Peter's falling asleep after Jesus had asked him to watch and pray.

"Put your sword away." This in response to Peter's valiant effort to defend Jesus and severing the ear of the servant of the high priest.

So, to put it simply, as it seems to me very likely, Peter was following from afar because he had his feelings hurt, maybe was even mad at Jesus. And so when the testing came, Peter failed. "I do not know the man."

But, the good news is that the failure wasn't final. A quick read of the first chapters of the book of Acts shows Peter in fine form, preaching boldly and thousands responding to his message of new life through the crucified and resurrected Christ.

And why wasn't his failure final? Three reasons come to mind.

First of all, Jesus told Peter before-hand that a special time of testing was coming for him, but that he had prayed for him, and no doubt continued to pray for him as the evening unfolded.

Secondly, in Mark's account of the resurrection, when the three women entered the empty tomb looking to anoint the body of Jesus and found the tomb empty, an angel of the Lord told them that Jesus was alive and to tell the disciples and Peter. Peter is the only disciple mentioned by name and is evidence that, while Peter may have been quick to forget Jesus, Jesus was not about to forget Peter.

And lastly, in John's account of the disciples going fishing after the resurrection, there is a wonderful exchange between Peter and Jesus. Three times Jesus asks Peter, "Do you love me?" And Jesus reinstates Peter in a wonderfully affirming way.

And so, while we may hold on to our hurt and anger over events real or imagined, in an effort to hurt our Lord, the only one we are truly hurting is ourselves. And though we may fail, and we all will sooner or later, we are believers in a Savior who loves us unconditionally, and unfailingly. And he has given his word, "I will never leave thee nor forsake thee!"

Made in the USA
Monee, IL
03 November 2020